CHAMPIONS
IN THE
MAKING

BOOK THREE: Ego States

J. ZINK, Ph.D.

OTHER PUBLICATIONS ON CHILD DEVELOPMENT

BY DR. ZINK:

CHAMPIONS IN THE MAKING
BOOK ONE: Building Positive Self-Concept in Kids (J. ZINK, INC., 1981)
(formerly titled *BREAKFAST FOR CHAMPIONS: BUILDING POSITIVE SELF-CONCEPT IN KIDS).*

CHAMPIONS IN THE MAKING
BOOK TWO: Motivating Kids (J. ZINK, INC., 1983)

CHAMPIONS ON THE SCHOOL BUS: A SCHOOL BUS DRIVER'S GUIDE TO POSITIVE DISCIPLINE ON THE SCHOOL BUS (J. ZINK, INC., 1982).

CHAMPIONS IN THE LIBRARY: A LIBRARIAN'S GUIDE TO POSITIVE DISCIPLINE IN THE LIBRARY (J. ZINK, INC., 1982).

CHAMPIONS IN THE MAKING: A POSITIVE APPROACH TO DISCIPLINE (AUDIO TAPE) J. ZINK, INC., 1982.

A POSITIVE APPROACH TO DISCIPLINE (VIDEO TAPE) J. ZINK, INC., 1982.

THE COMPLETE CHAMPIONS WORKSHOP (AUDIO TAPES) J. ZINK, INC., 1986.

CATCH 'EM DOING SOMETHING RIGHT!

Dr. J. ZINK

ISBN 0-942490-05-3

FIRST PRINTING, MAY, 1986
SECOND PRINTING, MAY, 1988

Special thanks to Len and Janet Davis for typing and printing this book.

Printed in U.S.A. by Iwate Printing, 13616 Normandie Ave., Gardena, CA 90247

This Book is For

KERN WALSH ZINK,

After twenty years of
marriage, I can say with
certitude, you are the
Perfect Adult Ego.

INTRODUCTION

I am writing this little book for several reasons worth mentioning here. First, I have encountered in my private practice what I call the "Ego State Problem" almost daily. I have witnessed the psychological carnage caused by the tyranical Parent Ego State. Furthermore, I have seen it at the beginning, during the traumatic middle stages, and watched it ultimately consume in bitterness, disillusion, and poor mental health its owner.

Secondly, I write because of the success I have enjoyed in redirecting the destructive energy of the parent ego into more constructive and positive expressions created by the growth, development, and strengthing of the adult ego.

The adult ego can be acquired. It can be studied, emulated, practiced, learned, and, ultimately, mastered. I count among my most intimate friends many former patients who studied the true wonder of the flowering of their own adult egos with me.

Finally, I write this book as a positive message to all parents and teachers who read it. Follow the steps I outline for you to take. Encourage this new change in you, love yourself greatly for the courage you have to want to change; DO NOT BE CRUSHED if you have a bad day, make a few bad choices, and fail. Remember, the ultimate knowledge of the adult ego state is expressed in the phrase "Failure is not permanent." To that wisdom, I add, "Success is forever when measured in feelings." And the true meaning of these words is the ultimate goal of my book. "Success is forever when measured in feelings" means that by forgiving yourself for the bad choices of the past, and by learning from these bad choices how to make good choices, your success and the impact of your success on your children, students, friends, associates, and all who are graced with the opportunity to meet you and know you insures that your life leaves a positive imprint in the sand on the beachhead of time. I want my print to be there right next to yours. And this book is one part of my imprint.

J. Zink, Ph.D.
Manhattan Beach,
California
May, 1986

CHAMPIONS IN THE MAKING

BOOK THREE: Ego States

J. ZINK, Ph.D.

An emotional resource book for parents and teachers.

TABLE OF CONTENTS

PAGE

Chapter One:

THE EMOTIONAL MEANING OF EGO STATE

In the past, my writings have relied very little on psychological terminology or jargon. I have much distrust for terms which seem to be indigenous to a particular profession. They have a way of saying, "I know what this means and you don't. This gives me power over you." Therefore, we nod our heads and pretend to fully understand when our physician (major offender of jargon control) says, "contraindications of drug usage," or our tax attorney (another jargon felon) talks about "minimizing bracket creep."

I am forced to use the potentially alienating term "ego state" throughout this book because that is what this book is about. If you nod your head throughout this book kidding yourself that you know what I mean when I use it, and you do not really **understand** it, then the full impact of my words on your own effort to master the adult ego state will be crippled. How can we master what we may not fully understand?

Therefore, I must teach you the meaning **I have** for the term ego state because my meaning (as opposed to someone else's) is the one upon which the specific ideas in this book are based. So, if you are currently holding **no meaning** for the term, you are at a greater advantage than someone who holds someone else's meaning (or their own) for the term, "ego state," because at least your mind is blank on the subject and (hopefully after all this discourse) ready to be enlightened. If you hold a meaning for the term, make an effort now to prepare to replace it.

EGO STATE DEFINED

Ego state is the feeling you have about yourself and others at any given moment. There are a thousand shades of gray here but for our work together in this book we will use those given to us by Eric Berne and, later, Thomas Harris as he refined the original concepts developed by Dr. Berne and ultimately called them "transactional analysis." The three ego states we will use are called parent, child, and adult.

Now instead of teaching the meaning of these terms to you **intellectually** with dictionary-like definitions, I will teach them to you **emotionally** which is, after all, the way you will express them. I suppose if your goal in life is to be a psychologist, then you would want to master the intellectual meaning of these terms (and millions of others) so you could impress yourself and others with your mastery of the subject. But if your goal is to be a more effective parent or a more competent teacher (which I presume it to be) then **forget** about intellectual definitions because these change with who's using the term. Concentrate on mastering the concepts **emotionally**. This way (as it is commonly said) you have a "good feel" for them. More on feelings, later.

I will give you a series of very familiar statements and follow these by stating which ego state produced them.

You'll get the idea very quickly. (Nice thing about the emotional mind, by the way, it usually learns with the speed of lightning.)

"Let me tell you something, young man. If you think I was born yesterday, you've got another thing coming."
(Parent Ego Statement)

"I don't know who did it. All I know is it wasn't me."
(Child Ego Statement)

"What are some steps we can all take to avoid this problem tomorrow?"
(Adult Ego Statement)

Do you see my point about the emotional mind? Now you have the concepts of the three ego states in your **emotional** mind because you experienced certain fascinating emotions as you read each sentence and **felt** your response to each one. If you did not, go back and read each one slowly and with feeling.

Here are some more, just for fun (which **is** learning, of course).

*"Good God. Am I the only one who does **anything** right in this house?"*

"You know, for two cents I'd leave every last one of you to fend for

---

yourselves. I just wonder how long you'd last."

"What did I do to deserve this? I worked and slaved and sacrificed every damn day of my life for you and this is the thanks I get!"
(Parent in the Parent Ego State)

"Is this your homework? Did you eat lunch on it?"

"When you learn how to work and pay attention in my class, and only then, will you get a passing grade from me."

"I'm a really nice person when you're nice to me, but if you cross me, watch out. That's all I can say, just watch out."
(Teacher in the Parent Ego State)

*"He hit me first. Why don't you ever believe **me**?"*

"I promise it will never happen again. Just give me one more chance, please."

"I don't want to hear it, mother. So save your breath. I don't even want to hear it."
(Child with a little Parent thrown in: "save your breath.")

"I didn't do it. It wasn't me."

"It didn't break."

"I promise I'll turn it in tomorrow."

"We don't have homework today."
(more Child Ego State)

"Michael, you've made a bad choice. You are having a bad day. Hang in there. We all have them. As we agreed, the price for your bad choice is 15 minutes in detention after school today. I hope your day tomorrow is better."
(Teacher in the Adult Ego State)

"David, I am impressed! This car looks like it did the day I drove it from the dealership. Thanks for the hard work in cleaning it. You help me feel so elegant when my car shines."
(Parent in the Adult Ego State)

"Thanks, Mom. I love it when you put spray starch on my shirts. They feel so crisp."
(Child in the Adult Ego State)

"I don't feel so good right now. I feel I let the team down. I let you down. I let myself down. I am sorry for the attitude. Forgive me."
(Child in the Adult Ego State.)

See how easy it is to learn emotionally! Did you notice that we **all** can exhibit all **three** ego states? Because children are people (we sometimes forget that), they can be in their Child, Parent, or Adult Ego State. And you're thinking (I hope), "I don't recall seeing an example of a child in a Parent Ego State." Good. I didn't give you a complete example. But here's a humdinger. (I hope it doesn't hurt — some of these can be painful, I know.)

"You're not my real mother. You're just some woman who sleeps with my father. You don't even care for him. You just like his money."
(Child in the Parent Ego State)

And now you understand **emotionally** what this book and my work are all about. For the true purpose of this work is to teach you emotionally how to identify your own Adult Ego State, learn how to express your Adult Ego State, get inside your Adult Ego State (it's very safe and wonderfully healthy there), and discover what a wonderful, complete, exciting, competent, loving, and **giving** person you are in the Adult Ego State.

In order to get you there and keep you there, we have to discover why you have a parent ego, when your child shows up, what you can do to avoid your child ego, and **how to turn your parent ego off**. I hope you are as excited as I am about the prospect. Learning is great fun and learning your Adult Ego State is one of the greatest inner adventures of all. My greatest goal for our work here is to be able to demonstrate unequivocally to you what a remarkable, wonderful, sensitive, loving, and **lovable** human being you are.

Chapter Two:

THE PARENT EGO STATE

Logic dictates, as Mr. Spock on *Star Trek* says, that we should begin with the Child Ego State since we are children before we are parents or teachers. However, we shall not confuse logic with emotional truth, for they very often are different. In this rare case, however, they are the very same. The Child Ego State is essentially a reactive and defensive emotional posture. It is not a good logical choice for a starting place. The Parent Ego State directly **causes** the Child Ego State (thank goodness!). So when we **change** the parent, we change the child. This is a wonderful rule for you to observe when contemplating all behavior change. The only person I can control **completely** is me. No one else. So, only as I change me, do I change you. No one will be affected **positively**, unless I change myself **positively**.

I have been in private practice for ten years, as a professional educational consultant, professional educator (for 18 years), and as a therapist certified by the State of California to practice clinical hypnosis on children. Only in ten percent of all the cases that I see is there a problem which belongs to the child alone. (For example, developmental dyslexia, attention deficit disorder with or without hyperactivity, etc.) The other ninety percent of the time the problem originates from and is directly caused by parents or teachers. The problem **is solved by** effecting specific behavior change in the parent or teacher.

So, the Parent Ego State is the most appropriate place to start. What is it? Where does it come from? And how does it do the damage it does? Most importantly, how can it be so powerful as to determine so much of the lack of happiness in children as they grow and develop? These are the questions we must squarely face and answer in this chapter.

The Parent Ego State is a feeling about oneself and others which is characterized by two words: **should** and **ought**. These words, when used by anyone toward us, indicate that we somehow are not living up to their expectations of us — that somehow we have failed them. That we have through our own deliberate or accidental actions greatly or minorly disappointed them. That for some reason we have become "bad" and that we are "not ok" in their esteem. There is something "wrong" with us. The Parent Ego State says we should or ought to have done something we did not do, or felt something we did not feel, or ought not to have done something we did, or should not have felt something we did feel. The Parent Ego State appoints itself as an expert in all or most matters related to living life and getting educated. It tells all who come into range where they made their mistake, went wrong, messed up, screwed up, **and does it with an attitude** which is essentially smug and artificially self-assured. The attitude is this, "I'm right and you're wrong. I win and you lose. I am a winner because I know how to do this and you are a loser because you don't. I know how to do this because I have lived all these years and you are young and silly. And even if you are as old as I am or older, I'm smarter. You wasted your life being stupid, but I am different from you. I am smart."

So one major emotional feature of the Parent Ego State is the insistence on the **differences** between us. The Parent Ego State only focuses on the similarities when it has a story to tell about how when I was your age, or I did that stupid thing once, too, but I (in contrast to you) smartened up. The implication is: **you should, too**. And there is that word, again. Should.

The statement is simple: I used to be as dumb or stupid or unenlightened or dull or ineffective (or whatever negative you want) but now we are **different**. I am smart, effective, efficient, competent, neat, rich, free, brave, sensible, etc., and you aren't. I know this and you don't. This gives me the right to tell you how to live your life.

Parents have Parent Ego. Teachers have Parent Ego. Institutions (made up of individuals) can have Parent Ego (schools and prisons come to mind), and even countries can have Parent Ego. "When we kill your people, it is to preserve freedom. When you kill our people, it is because you are bloodthirsty, evil, illigitimate children of Satan and you're too stupid and savage to know any better."

The Parent Ego says, "I am killing you because you are too stupid to learn this lesson." The Parent Ego State, then, explains war. That it does so simply does not surprise me since war is essentially the most profound human manifestation of destruction. The Parent Ego State, even when **not** carried to its logical extreme, is essentially destructive. It is a destructive force among humans and what it destroys is their ability to emotionally bond and love each other. The irony is that we have so many parents and teachers who **intellectually** believe in truth, justice, freedom, equality, democracy, love, and other lofty principles and who **emotionally** use their Parent Ego States to punish, repress, enslave, frighten, and yes, derange children under the belief that they are using good, sound, and old-fashioned discipline. "I'll teach you a thing or two, young lady," or as the pathetic school administrator in the film *Breakfast Club* says so perfectly, "I'll show you, young man. You mess with the bull, you'll get the horns."

Understanding the what of the Parent Ego State, in short, is simple. With practice, you can identify it first in others (easy) and then in yourself (harder) but understanding the why of the Parent Ego State is a litte more complex. Why do we have a Parent Ego State? Where does it come from? And, what purpose, if any, does it serve?

Let's focus on why we have this state first. Again, the answer is simple. We have a Parent Ego State because we have parents. We got it from them. And, the stronger theirs is (was), the stronger ours is. The more damage they did to us with theirs, the greater the likelihood that we will continue the vicious cycle on our children. Unless, of course, our parents had strong Adult Ego States to balance their inadvertent attack with love. Ah, the offsetting and saving grace of the Adult Ego. But that is the matter of a later chapter. For now, consider the problem which is central to all parents and teachers: How to get children to do what they don't want to do. For most parents and teachers, the Parent Ego State provides the most immediate (if ineffective and irresolute) solution to this central problem. "I'll just tell them what they **should** be doing." "Avenge me." Hamlet's father's ghost tells poor young Hamlet. "If ever thou didst thy poor father love, avenge me." Nice guy, Hamlet's father. A gem. No wonder Shakespeare has him appear in chains and smelling of hell fire. The play *Hamlet* is replete with powerful ironies, since Hamlet spends the whole play torturing himself with what he **should** be doing. What he should be doing is the question more central to the play than to be or not to be since ultimately Hamlet must decide to live up to his own or to **his father's** expectations. But while there is a lot of his father, the king, in him, there is not quite enough for the young prince to make his own decisions and be his own person in a kingly fashion. His need to defend himself from his mother is strong. Gertrude is one supreme example in English literature of the Parent Ego State's destructive prowess. And in telling her son how he **should** behave she has no more luck than we do in getting our children or students to clean up their rooms or do their homework when they want to do something else. "I don't **feel** like it," they say.

So we hear coming **out of our mouths** our parent's

own words. And, as it should be, this is so punishing (for everyone!). So when they say, "I don't feel like it," we say, "What's to feel? Get in there and clean up your room right now! Do you hear me? Do I make myself clear?" Even as I write these words I hear them in my head being spoken but not in my voice. I hear them in my father's voice (of course!). Knowing my father, I suspect he hears the same words but in his mother's voice.

Essentially, if we are plagued by a powerful Parent Ego State, we have a vast library of behavioral directives and beliefs stored in our subconscious minds ready to spring forth at the right moment of stimulation. Nothing stimulates production of these sophisms, clichés, platitudes, and general directions on life like the sight of a kid who is floundering. And thus was it ever from generation to generation. In the Sixteenth Century it was father Polonius, to son Laertes, in *Hamlet*: "Neither a borrower nor a lender be." Today it is: "No daughter of mine is leaving this house dressed like that!" The same statement was made in the twenties by fathers of "flappers," in the forties by fathers of "zoot-suiters," in the sixties by fathers of "hippies," and in the eighties by fathers of "punkers."

Of course, students leaving home to go to school (Laertes) or flappers, zoot-suiters, hippies, and punkers all wanted and needed attention. What they really wanted and needed was Adult Ego State acceptance and approval but since they ("I can't get no satifaction") couldn't find any, they all settled for a good drubbing (Chicago, 1968,

"The whole world's watching") of Parent Ego State (Mayor Daley, father figure, asks "What trees do they plant?") because, no matter how painful, **Parent Ego State attention is better than no Ego State at all**. As a twelve year old patient of mine said once: "I know why you scream at me, mother. You really care but you don't know how to say it."

How comforting.

So now you see the only legitimate value of the Parent Ego. It is better than nothing. The emotional logic goes like this: As long as you're beating me, I know this: You must care about something to put this much energy and emotion into it. I sure hope I'm the something you care about even though you have a strange way of saying, "I love you." When you think about it, we have arrived at a wonderfully functional definition of the Parent Ego State: A strange way of saying "I care."

Another hallmark of the Parent Ego State is the fundamental paradox of child rearing and teaching. Somehow we believe that we can teach children to control their behavior by losing control of ours. We nag (OK, "Remind" is your word) them to feed the dog, get back to their seat, pick up the crayons, eat their peas, don't bite their fingernails, stop smoking, put the toilet seat up (or down), throw the empty package away, raise your hand before you speak in my class, and a million other habituated behaviors by using an habituated behavior (nagging) ourselves. Then we are exasperated when it does not work.

Actually, we are often more than exasperated. We become deadly. Because when we see how ineffective we are, we turn our Parent Ego State on ourselves. The little voice (nagging) turns from them to us. It sounds like this: "It's all my fault, I suppose. It all started with the divorce." Or, "Here I am a teacher in this district and my own children are failing in school. My God, how humiliating!"

Of course, we can only take so much blame and guilt from the parent inside us. And the parent is always looking for someone to blame. "Who did this? Look at what some kid did now. My God, how I dream about waking up some day and walking into my kitchen to find it clean. No dirty dishes, no juice spilled on the counter, no dog food all over the floor, no filthy butts in the ashtray. God, I dream of this but it'll never happen around here. No."

Then surfeited with feeling sorry for ourselves, we blame others. Like the school district. "More paperwork. Are you kidding? Do those people know we teach children here. Let them hire a secretary." We blame the principal. "That man, honey, is trouble. I can't stand to look into his beady little eyes." And, of course, we blame our spouses. "Let me get this straight. You have a college education. You wrote a check knowing there was no money in the account."

The better educated we are, it seems, the more

dangerous our Parent Ego State becomes. Now we have the precise language and succinct descriptors with which to prosecute. "And armed with this specific knowledge, you deliberately and cold-bloodedly fed the amphetamine to the innocent and defenseless animal. You make me sick with disgust. What we have here, ladies and gentlemen, is a nine-year-old parakeet killer. A revolting little future Charles Manson. Get into your room, I don't want to see your face. As far as I am concerned, you are grounded for the rest of your miserable and pathetic life." Come to think of it, so is Charles Manson.

When there are two parents in the family and one has a more pronounced Parent Ego State, the other often is forced to side with the child and defend what often is hard to defend. Then we see the spectacle of a family which is a non-family shredded and tattered psychologically into camps and factions. It is the haunting tragedy of a group of human beings struggling more to survive from each other than the world.

Then enter substance abuse. Drug and alcohol use very often is high among heavy Parent Ego States. These substances are abused because they serve to temporarily deactivate the torturing voice of the Parent Ego. "Christ, I don't care what the hell the snot does. We'll have a drink together and laugh about it someday. Get me another cold one, will ya, hon?"

Then enter mental illness in one or more of its variant

manifestations. Violence to self or others is born of a
desire to punish or blame. Exacting some real or symbolic
retribution on the self or others is the tortured psyche's
way to strike back. It is as if we are symbolically aligned
with Melville's captain Ahab — a truly sick man if there
ever was one. Ahab seeks to blame all the ills of the world
and the misery of his life on one symbolic evil, the white
whale. For by killing this symbol, he punishes and
destroys all who have ever hurt him, maimed him, re-
duced his self-esteem and stature in his own eyes and the
taunting, accusing eyes of others. For when we seek to
destroy ourselves, others, like Ahab's crew, go down with
us. Perhaps this is why Ahab baptizes his harpoon in fire
and blood and says, *"Ego non baptizo te in nomine patris, sed in
nomine diaboli."* I baptize you not in the name of the father,
but in the name of the devil. Did you notice the Latin
word for "I" is "Ego"? Splendid.

The most prominent expression of the Parent Ego is the
desire to punish. This is why the Parent Ego resorts to the
rod, the razor strap, the pancake turner, a spoon, the back
of the hand, a good shaking, stand in the corner, a good
swift kick in the pants, a piece of my mind, a knuckle
sandwich, a smack in the chops, a rap across the bridge of
the nose, or a belt to enforce its point. It is the old Hebrew
law of *Lex Talionis*, the law of retribution or revenge,
which says an eye for an eye and a tooth for a tooth. The
medieval concept of wergild, which means man-gold, or if
you kill a man you must replace his value to his lord or his

family with money, is another historical form of the Parent Ego State. This concept represents a historical change in the socio-historical development of the Parent Ego. But as it was employed in the Middle Ages in Europe, it was more a punishment and deterrent rather than a moral consequence of a bad choice.

A final hallmark of the Parent Ego State is the insistent predilection of the Parent Ego to accept emotional responsibility for the behavior of others. The Parent Ego says: We are different (but they aren't!) and it's my fault. Whatever my child or my student does reflects on me. This is especially true when what the child does is a bad choice. My students' test scores are low so I must be a bad teacher, the logic goes. Or, my son is smoking dope and it's all my fault. So, psychologically, the need to punish a child is really a **subconscious desire to punish the self**. Since I have been using the word punish for some time, I feel a need to define it **precisely** in emotional terms so that we can continue working toward an emotional understanding of the Parent Ego. Punishment is anytime anyone says or does something that makes another person, **or themselves**, feel bad about themselves as a person. Anything that is demeaning, degrading, humiliating, physically painful, emotionally painful, or sexually painful is punishment. Real illness begins in us when we learn to love the pain because we find it superior to no feeling at all. Although there are exceptions to this definition of punishment (physical pain caused by heart surgery, mental anguish caused by psychotherapy, etc.), we will use this definition as the basis for our discussion of why the Parent Ego State does so much damage.

My favorite psychotherapeutic model (read *"Mental Health Image"*) for describing how our self-concepts are formed is to imagine that as people we are all born as beautiful barrels. Our barrels are capable of holding and filling up with love. Our barrels hold self-respect, self-esteem, respect for authority, love for ourselves, love for others, and more because we are all unique expressions of individual energy in the universe. The thicknesses of our barrels differ. Some children are born with bottoms on their barrels which are made from six inches of solid oak. No matter what attacks they suffer from the Parent Ego States of others, they withstand the onslaught. Their barrels maintain their structural integrity even though they never know their own father and their mothers are hookers and drug addicts. These children grow up on their own, get a scholarship, and take an M.B.A. from Wharton, Berkeley, or Harvard. The research has a name for these children. It calls them Superkids.

Unfortunately, superkids are not the norm. Most of us have average thicknesses to our barrels and a lot of children have barrels made of *papier maché*. So every attack (even those done "for your own good") leaves a hole or two in the barrel. The Parent Ego, motivated by a desire to "Teach those kids a thing or two, by God," actually ruptures the youngster's barrel by lodging deep in their subconscious minds **the feeling** that they are somehow "not right" because they made Mother cry, or Dad mad, or the teacher shout at them.

You really do not have to be a Wharton graduate to figure out that a given barrel can take only so many penetrations of its integrity before it leaks. Frankly, although it may sound humorous, I am very serious when I say this is why we have so many enuretic children. They wet the bed in a symbolic gesture. It is a graphic depiction of their emotional situation. Barrels with holes do not fill up with love, affection, good feelings, enthusiasm for life and learning, and wonderful self-esteem. Barrels with holes just leak. And their owners feel empty. Sometimes their owners overeat in a dramatic and symbolic gesture. Sometimes their owners binge and then purge their bodies of food in an even more violent and symbolic gesture. But one thing is certain, you can't fill up a barrel which leaks, so don't expect love and unconditional approval from an empty barrel. They can't give what they don't have.

This is why children who have been subjected to someone's Parent Ego State have such low self-esteem, poor self-respect, and little self-love. This is why they avoid your eyes, mumble, refuse to participate, have no friends, and say, "I can't draw good," when you ask them to draw a picture of themselves. It explains why they often draw themselves without body parts (especially arms) and it is so sad to see a youngster draw Mother or Dad with no arms. It is alarming to see one draw parents with boxing gloves on their hands or spikes on their feet when they play no sports.

Some parents ask me why is it that one child is so good and the other one is so out of control. Of course, the metaphor of the barrel helps to explain the differences. Some children have thinner barrels than others. But there is another reason as well. Parents have different relationships with their children, too. Some children just naturally draw out the extremes of the Parent Ego State in their parents. One mother stood in the foyer to my office and introduced her two children to me. "This is David," she said, "David's my star. And this," she said, pointing to her little girl who looked down at the floor and clung pitifully to her mother's leg, "is Sheila. Sheila was God's nasty little surprise." It took the full force of my own Adult Ego State and complete therapeutic personality to restrain myself from strangling the woman on the spot. And don't I have the precise terminology to execute this lady with words! Instead I said, "Hello Sheila. Thank you for coming to visit me today." In the chapter on Adult Ego, I will describe what else I did to control my outrage. In fact, I will teach it to you so that you, too, may learn my secrets of turning off the Parent Ego. It can be done.

One final comment before we leave the Parent Ego and consider its partner in the destruction of self-esteem, the Child Ego State. Some professions are Parent Ego prone. One thinks of policemen, prosecuting attorneys, judges, penitentiary guards, detectives, IRS agents, customs officials, security personnel, newspaper and other media investigative reporters, to name a few. Isn't it odd that teachers don't immediately spring to mind. Yet we, colleagues, are among the worst offenders. Isn't it sad, too, because of all the above-named professions, we spend the most time with kids. Research has repeatedly demonstrated that the children remember us more for **how** we teach them rather than **what** we teach them. And each year, with the advent of the pre-school movement, single parent families (1 in 4 American families are now headed by a single parent), and the growth of the day-care phenomenon, we are spending more time with the children.

In closing our discussion of Parent Ego for now, I would like to call your attention to one prominent American who works with children every day and has no visible Parent Ego State. None. It is the reason, in my professional opinion, why millions of children love him, are devoted to him, freely quote him, and run to him when they hear his music and his voice. Of course, I speak of Fred Rogers and his *Mister Rogers' Neighborhood*. The reason? Ask the kids. They will tell you, "Mister Rogers loves me just the way I am." And he does. He very well does.

Notes

Chapter Three:

THE CHILD EGO STATE

Isaac Newton said it best. "For every action there is an equal and opposite reaction." While this forms one leg of the three-legged stool which is the foundation of Newtonian physics, this particular leg succinctly defines the underlying principle of the Child Ego. It is essentially reactive. To understand it fully we must return to the metaphor of the barrel. Children are people, remember, and like all people they have pronounced emotional needs. They need to be loved and appreciated. They need to be hugged and squeezed and tickled. They need to laugh with someone and hear wonderful stories which excite the creative force of their imaginations. They need to believe in something. If we fail to give them something to believe in, they will invent beliefs of their own. Most importantly, they need to believe that they are lovable. This belief alone has the power to fill their barrels. As their barrels fill, they give back their love to us in magical and blessed ways. The feeling we get from their returned love is unequaled in the whole fabric of the human experience. The returned love of a child touches us more deeply and more emotionally than almost any other form of love. This is because, I suppose, we realize how dependent that child is upon us for total survival. This is why the loss of a child affects parents with a human grief which time often fails to diminish. Parents who have lost a child have a way of letting you know this less than five minutes after you meet them. It is as if their Parent Ego States have condemned them to imprisonment for life. Like Sisyphus in the Greek myth they push the huge boulder of grief steadily up an increasingly steep mountain until of its own weight the boulder rolls down over them. Sadly they climb down the mountain and retrieve their beloved burden and start the push all over again.

The child whose barrel has been ruptured with "you're not ok" messages seeks desperately to fill up with parental approval. New research suggests that in the fifth month from conception until the 72nd month after birth more than 75 % of a child's brain dies and is regenerated by new cell growth. At no other time in a human's life does this phenomenon occur to this dramatic degree. Theorists on cognition (Read: *Thinking and Learning Specialists*) speculate that this remarkable metamorphosis takes place because the child's personality and basic tools for information gathering are being formed at a tremendous speed. If the human brain has, as some say, a billion brain cells (some say more, but whose counting), then 750 million of them die and are replaced in 76 months. Into this dramatic susceptability for change we introduce the two most important human beings in the world (Mom and Dad) and those other big persons *in loco parentis* (Latin for "parents make you crazy" — just kidding) Mrs. Johnson (day care), Mrs. Smith (kindergarten), and Mrs. Suarez (first grade), all telling the child what to do, ("Now we are going to color!"), how to do it, ("Stay in the lines!"), when to do it, ("No Trevor, we will play with the ball, later. Now we are coloring!"), and why to do it ("Because I said so, that's

why!"). With all those other kids in the center, personaliz-
ed attention is very rare. "When Mom picks me up at 6:30
pm, she is tired. We eat and go to bed, 'cause she is sleepy.
Sometimes I get a story. I wish she didn't have to go to
work all the time. Sometimes she cries after she thinks I'm
asleep. But I know she's been crying. Her eyes are always
red." Sometimes my little patients tell me the saddest
stories.

Teachers will tell you that American children have
changed dramatically in the last ten years. They will tell
you that this current generation of American children is
the rudest, most obnoxious, most defiant, most foul-
mouthed, most overly sexual, least kind, and most intense-
ly uncaring generation of children they ever have taught.

Sociologists tell us that in 1955 in America, one out of
every 35 American children was being raised by a single
parent. In 1986, one out of every four American children
are growing up in a single-parent family. Often our
children have had to lose their natural father from the
household and a disproportionately alarming number
have had to face the loss of one or more step-parents. This
loss shows itself directly in school, social, and academic
behavior. As teachers, we know almost immediately
when something bad has happened at home. It shows **the
very day** in the child's behavior. It has gotten so severe a
problem that most teachers will say. "Show me a child
whose A and B work drops dramatically to D and F and I'll
show you a divorce every time."

Because children are so reactionary, their behaviors are barometers for the emotional atmosphere around them. The Child Ego State says, "Accept me, love me, approve of me, and give me all the attention you can because I very much need to know I am lovable." In essence, the child says, "Fill up my barrel because it's big and dark and empty and scary." Here's how they say it: "Mommy, can I sleep with you, tonight? I'm scared. The monster is going to get me."

As we all know, children have magnificent imaginations. This is because they function so often in their subconscious minds. Children are easily hypnotized because their critical, intellectual conscious minds are yet to develop fully. Because they are so susceptible to suggestion, we who live our lives in the presence of children must be very careful not to give them a negative suggestion about themselves. Negative suggestions can emotionally cripple a child. Those critical 72 months of the first six years are times when the child is especially vulnerable to negative suggestions like, "What is wrong with you? Do you hear me? You're a bad boy!" "What! My little girl wouldn't leave such a mess. You must not be my little girl. Maybe I got somebody else's baby at the hospital!" "You do that one more time and I'll beat you bloody, do you understand?" These terrifying messages are brought to you by your friendly local Parent Ego State. They are all uttered with the utmost conviction (a good word!) and said with intensifying body language to drive the point deep **and forever** into the recording and non-filtering subconscious mind of the child. Remember now that the subconscious mind has no filters and it places no qualifiers next to these brutal impressions. The conscious, not the subconscoius, mind can say, "Oh mother's having a rough day. She's upset and she doesn't mean to suggest that I'm not really her child." In fact, and as we said earlier, the conscious mind and critical, discriminating factors of the child's conscious mind are very, very underdeveloped at ages six and below. On the other hand, the subconscious mind — the mind of the imagination with pirates, and spaceships, and Captain Kirk, and He-Man, and Voltron is extremely well developed. It never says "What a bunch of baloney." It simply records, and records, and records. And it never forgets what it records.

By now I hope you are beginning to discover the terror of a child growing up under the influence of a scolding, disapproving, critical, demanding, oppressive, and occasionally violent Parent Ego. Talk about no fun. What you need you don't get; what you don't want, you get plenty. The frustration of not being able to get their emotional needs met directly causes the loss of self-esteem and self-confidence. It leads many children to anger. They express this anger in emotional outbursts because they learned how to explode by observing the Parent Ego State in their parents. They become "difficult children." We give them labels and little else. We call them behavior disordered or severely behavior disordered. We call them "the problem child" and they live up to their negatively suggestive names. We even give them drugs to calm them down. Pill pushing pediatricians, lacking the training and skill to deal effectively with these "problem children," use what the drug companies are happy to provide. So, they ask for love, affection, attention, and emotional support; we give them Ritalin and Cylert and other amphetamines. Physicians praise what they euphemistically call the "paradoxical effect" of speed. They say on the street "speed kills," but in the sanctuary of the doctor's office speed is praised for its "paradoxical effect." It calms them down and no one knows why.

We could ask why are they so "hyper" in the first place. An excellent question I will not dodge. Have you ever watched someone in extreme need who cannot satisfy that need? They appear restless, agitated, motorized, and on-edge. They are nervous. Like an addict needing the reassurance of a fix or an alcoholic needing the encouragement of a stiff drink, children who are hyper, in my professional opinion, are in desperate straits for the reassuring and calming influence of warm, loving, and tender one-on-one human communication. Having taught self-hypnosis to thousands of "hyper" children over the past decade, I watch them calm and relax their extreme motor activity as my voice reassures them that my total attention is focused on them and their needs. Then, a beautiful thing usually happens. As they relax and enjoy our conversation, they leave their Child Ego State and become remarkably sophisticated children in their Adult Egos. Some of my most professionally enlightening and personally satisfying moments have occurred while conversing with children. Children say and do the most remarkable things, but usually not when you're treating them like kids. These magic moments usually happen when you are treating them like the curious, wonder-filled, and accepting, loving human beings they are. For as soon as you go into your Adult Ego, **so do they**. This, of course, is the secret of *Mister Rogers* and all those other adults who enjoy, love, inspire, and are loved by children.

Put another way, we have the instant and commanding power to keep them from whining, whimpering, screaming, running out of the room, slamming the door, yelling "I hate you! I hate you!," throwing themselves on the floor, punching their sisters, poisoning the parakeet, urinating in the water pistol, and all those millions of other Child Ego State behaviors that are simply their way of saying, "HELP." We have the power, yes. But learning how to use it is one of life's greatest challenges because when we do learn, we have finally learned how to truly do what our parent's Parents Ego States have been yelling at us to do all along: Grow up.

And finally growing up is what the Adult Ego State is all about.

Chapter Four:

THE ADULT EGO STATE

Our Adult Ego State is born the day we realize we must accept full responsibility for all of our own actions and we cannot accept responsibility for the actions of others. Unfortunately, not everyone's Adult Ego gets to be born because some people never come fully to the realization that they must mark their own scorecard and they can't mark anyone else's. The Adult Ego recognizes by its behavior that it can only change itself. True control comes from within and the only discipline is self-discipline. This form of self-control exerts a staggeringly powerful influence over others and teaches them, by example, how to control and be responsible for themselves. This is why the Adult Ego State affects children so positively. They learn to control and discipline themselves by watching you control and discipline yourself.

If you say what you mean and mean what you say, they respect you. You explain to them the rules for your classroom, and tell them if they make bad choice and break a rule, **they** choose to pay a price. Such a price can be the loss of a privilege, an extra assignment, detention, in general, anything which is boring. Children hate to be bored. If you tell them your job is to catch them making good choices and give them your sincere, personal attention, even if only for a few seconds, they will behave for you even when they behave for no one else. Because they respect, love, and admire you. And they like how they feel in your presence.

I have been teaching this positive approach to discipline

for over ten years to more than a million parents and
teachers in forty-five states and five countries. No one has
yet to say to me, "It doesn't work." And now you know
why. Because the "program of classroom management and
home discipline" I teach is nothing more than this: A step-
by-step formula for learning your Adult Ego State and
how to stay in it.

Our work in this chapter is to examine carefully the
magic and the wonder of the Adult Ego. We must gently
disassemble it in order to understand its various com-
ponents. After we reassemble it because we understand it
intellectually, then I will re-teach it to you **emotionally**.
Only then do I want you to begin to wear it and get comfortable with it. We shall break it in slowly and with the
tenderness and admiration it deserves. If it feels a little un-
comfortable at first — perhaps a little awkward, that's OK.
It is only a little stiff because it is new. St. Paul urged the
Corinthians to "Put on the new man." And so I will urge
you to do the same. If it takes a little time to get used to,
that's OK, too. My dear friend and esteemed colleague,
Dr. Marjorie Barlow of Kingsville and Corpus Christi,
Texas, says, "Fake it until you make it." And you will
make it. I believe you will or I would be wasting my time
writing this book. The Italian poet Dante Alighieri said
that love only comes to a gentle heart. And when he first
saw his beloved Beatrice, he said in Latin, *"Incepit vita
nuova,"* which means, "Here begins the new life." If you
long for a new life with a gentle, loving heart, then the

Adult Ego State will give you a safe path for your journey. The journey must begin in your childhood.

The first major feature of the Adult Ego State is that it accepts the fortunes and misfortunes of childhood. The Adult Ego recognizes that it cannot change what happened in the past, but it can, with a loving and less critical eye, reinterpret the disappointments and traumas of childhood by attempting to understand those events with an adult mind. Yes, I never got the full drum set I really wanted but that doesn't mean my parents didn't love me. They probably didn't have the $200 bucks. Or, yes, we didn't see much of the old man in those days but probably because he was hustling to make ends meet. Or, I don't know what caused my mother to say such a thing to me but she was under a lot of pressure, her only sister was dying of cancer, and she wasn't fairing too well with my father in those days. Or, I can't imagine what possessed Sister Philomena to do such a thing to a little innocent kid like I was, but the lady was suffering terribly when she found out that the church had decided there was no Saint Philomena.

Forgiving the Parent Ego States of your past is an effective way to start getting rid of your own Parent Ego. Remember, they were so hard on you because someone was hard on them and they were suffering. Realize now that while they were yelling and screaming or ignoring you, they were dealing with their own ghosts. You came along and **painfully** reminded them of their own mistakes.

So they got upset with you because they decided that God put them on earth to save you from suffering the way they did. And they lived out the life script they were given — only realizing they were part of the problem when it was too late. Your relationship with them was in ruins. So forgive them all now.

They were doing the best job they knew how to do. And you can forgive them. You can.

Another major feature of the Adult Ego State is the desire to get its needs met without violating the rights of others. This is why I teach parents and teachers to get their basic human needs met in the form of rules. Sometimes my patients who are parents ask me, "But when I state my rules am I in my Parent Ego or my Adult?"

A fine question. The answer, of course, is Adult. The Parent Ego doesn't make any rules until it sees you do something it considers dumb, stupid, or ridiculous. Then it climbs all over you. The Adult Ego says, "This is my house (or classroom) and here are my needs. The way to build a meaningful relationship with me is to respect my needs as a person. I will respect your needs for food, clothing, shelter, warmth, love, positive attention, and education. In this way we will be emotionally bonded."

Sigmund Freud used the Greek word *"cathexis,"* to describe this wonderful human bonding in love. We *cathect* with children when we tell them how to please us (rules) and respond with enthusiasm and emotion when they do.

Only Adult Egos can *cathect*.

When we ensure that children pay a price for breaking the rules because **they** chose to pay that price (loss of TV, stereo, right to have a friend stay the night, etc.), **and we are still loving**, emotionally supportive and understanding that they are having a bad day, then we say by our behavior that, no matter what, we will always love them. And we are not the judge, jury, and lord high executioner. In fact, we are empathetic **but not upset**. Why? Because the Adult Ego State does not take their bad choices personally. The Adult Ego says it's OK to make a bad choice because **that is how we learn**.

Sure, you are going to be upset if one of your children runs out in front of a car. You'll probably yell. Of course, you will be terribly disturbed if you walk in your son's bedroom and he is playing with your husband's loaded revolver. And, yes, you will be emotionally shaken when you walk into your classroom and discover two of your fourth graders masturbating each other.

But think about if for a minute. What purpose is served by your tirade, lecture, display of anger, frustration, or fury? The answer is none. In the case of the sex offenders, your reaction may well serve to traumatize them into patterns of dysfuntional sexual behavior later. In the case of the revolver, you may scare him into pulling the trigger. In the case of the car in the street, your horror may paralyze her into a panic freeze in the vehicle's path.

The Adult Ego reacts to each of these situations with a measured response designed to first communicate your emotions by **telling** your fears **not showing** them. This quiet communication takes ten seconds. You say, "Colin, when I saw you in the street in front of the car I was very frightened." Probably then he will say, "Me, too, Mom." If you scream at him, he will cast his eyes down and repress the opportunity to express his own feelings.

Then you say, "Colin, from now on we have this rule. You must not cross the street without first looking in both directions."

Then you ask him, "Colin, what is the new rule?" You think he will think you think he is stupid because you are asking him to repeat what you just said. He won't think this. He will repeat the rule. "The new rule is that I must look both ways before crossing the street."

Then you say, "Excellent. You got it right the first time. You have very good listening skills and a good memory. Now, close your eyes and see the words in your mind as you say them (if he can read, of course). Say them very slowly."

Colin closes his eyes and says the new rule slowly. You praise him for following directions. Then you ask, "Did you see the words?" He says. "Yes, Mom, I did."

You say, "Good. Now, if you make a bad choice and forget and break the rule by just walking or running into the street, **you will have chosen** to go to bed that evening after supper with the lights out (night lite is ok, of course) and no television or radio. This is the price for your bad choice. Now, tell me what happens when you break the street rule?"

He says, "I go to bed early with the lights out. No TV. No radio."

You say, "You are correct, Colin."

He says, "Mom?"

"Yes?"

"Could you read me a story, though, if I can't watch TV or listen to my radio?"

You say, "No."

Then you say, "If you make a good choice and I catch you looking both ways before you cross the street, then that night I will tell you **two** stories before you go to bed. And one story will be about me when I was a little girl."

Colin says, "Goody. I love those stories."

Now you are learning how the Adult Ego handles the trauma of children running out in the street without looking.

Sounds like some work, doesn't it? It is. It is the most important work you'll ever do. What is more important than raising your children? I can think of nothing. It is **worth** the hard work.

Do you know how the Parent Ego handles this problem? Sure you do. "Colin, if you ever do that again and by some miracle the car doesn't kill you, I will. Do you understand me! ! !" (Often accompanied by grabbing and shaking.)

Quite a difference, isn't there?

In the Parent Ego, we have one-way communication. You talk and they listen while you dump on them. They are not equipped to handle your emotional outbursts. This is why they are so quiet, sullen, and avoid your eyes. They don't know what to say. This silence angers you, so you shout, "Look at me when I talk to you," or you ask the questions to which there is no answer like, "Just what am I supposed to do about this?"

"Answer me!" You shout. And they **always** say the same sentence (which is the truth, by the way):

"I don't know."

The Adult Ego artfully engages them in a meaningful dialogue and actively encourages them to participate in a limited and safe way in the solution. It also sensitizes them to your concerns and presents **A Plan of Action** for dealing with the problem in the future.

Plans of action are a major nuance of the Adult Ego. Adults are always making plans to get their needs met. Parent Egos get angry and seek someone to blame; Adult Egos **use less energy** to make a plan of action than it takes to stomp around like a wounded buffalo (as my beloved father loves to say). So, the choice is yours. You can use your limited energy to thunder (full of sound and fury signifying nothing) or you can use your energy to develop, with Colin's participation, a plan of action. This latter choice includes the elegant advantage of modeling for Colin how adults cope with an increasingly complex world. They get a plan and if that plan doesn't work, as Paul Simon says, "They make a new plan, Stan."

Please notice, too, that mother's plan of action for Colin did not involve making Colin pay a price for the **initial** sensitizing event. I am against creating a price on the spot and making them pay it when they didn't know about it **in advance**. You see, the fifth amendment to the Constitution of the United States guarantees due process of the law. The theory of due process says we all have the right to know about the consequence **before** we break the law. This is to prevent arbitrary imprisonment by overzealous Parent Ego States just looking for someone to punish.

We must keep this in mind, too. The beauty of a plan of action is that it is devised in the cool light of reason, not the heat of frustration and passion. Such prices devised on the spot are usually punishment. They are often so irrational that the children ignore them and after a while so do you.

You say in anger, "All right, Mr. Smart Guy, just for that no dinner for a month." It never works.

Now it is time to consider the importance of choices in your positive plan of action. The Adult Ego loves choices. It recognizes that life is a never ending (almost) series of behavioral choices. We make good ones and we **feel** good. Emotionally, we learn to make good choices. When we make bad choices, we **feel** bad. Emotionally, we learn how to avoid bad choices and make ones which help us feel better. Of all people, Ernest Hemingway once defined basic human morality this way. He said, more or less, that if after you did something you felt good, then it was good. And if after you did it, you felt bad, then it was bad. I like this simple approach to the complex subject of morality because of the emphasis it places on choices **and** feelings. It is almost always true that as long as you are in touch with your feelings and can even halfway articulate them, your mental health is sound. But if you start ignoring, suppressing, or repressing (when you repress you can't remember them consciously) then you are getting into trouble.

In the example of Colin and his mom above, you can see how Mom's calm, relaxed Adult Ego gave Colin the opportunity to express his own fears and concerns for his safety. This is healthy for Colin. And so good for Mom. The proof is how she feels about herself as a mother after sharing her plan and feelings with her son. She feels good. She feels competent. And she feels that she has made a good choice by coming to terms with her emotions, sharing them with her son, and devising a plan to respond to the problem in the future. Hemingway's simple definition of morality works nicely for both mom and Colin. Mom turned a potentially unpleasant situation for both mother and son into an essentially positive exchange. This exchange brings them closer emotionally because Mom recognizes that she cannot control Colin's behavior. There is nothing she can do, short of tying him up like a dog on a leash, locking him in the house, or what most Parent Egos do, NAG, NAG, NAG, to keep Colin from running in the street without looking if he chooses to do so. Mom does recognize that she can control her own behavior and this is precisely what she does as she remains calm, shares her feelings, develops a plan, and communicates that plan to her son.

She has given Colin, also, a wonderful way to earn her positive attention in the future. She has told him that she intends to catch him being good and that she will be watching for him to make a good choice and look both ways before crossing. Now Colin will wait to make sure she is watching before he deliberately and with extreme head gestures looks both ways before he crosses. Mom will praise this behavior. She will read or invent two stories that night. One will be how she learned to make good choices as a child and Colin will listen with keen fascination because children love to hear stories about the childhood of their parents. It is so very hard to imagine Mom as a little girl, Colin will say, and mother will say that she looked just like him only she wasn't as cute. Colin will say "Yuk" and go to sleep.

The Adult Ego State is largely non-judgmental. It does not seek to defend, offend, redress, rectify, or prosecute. It

asks only to be allowed to love, appreciate, emotionally
support, be amused, and amuse. It sees humor in
everything and people who have a good sense of humor
usually have well-defined and clearly observable Adult
Egos. Their humor is often at the general condition rather
than at someones's expense. If it is at someone's expense,
usually an unspoken agreement about the use of humor
and the misuse of humor has been informally established
between the communicators. For humor can be a vicious
and unrelenting tool of the Parent Ego. Unguarded and
unrefined, pointed humor and finely honed wit can rake
over another person's self-esteem and leave it scarred.
Parents who do this to children get their reward in the
end; their children avoid them as adults. Teachers who use
humor to attack children do not belong in our profession.
Period.

But the teachers whose sense of timing and humorous
manner make learning light-hearted and enjoyable are the
most talented members of our profession. Because emotional bonds form between children in their Adult Egos
and teachers in their Adult Ego when they share a
hilarious moment. And the learning process is intensified.
Also, remember that humor is an emotion. Watch a person crying and laughing and you discover that they use
the same facial muscles to do both. Getting children to
laugh relaxes them, puts them at ease, breaks down ten-
sions, and opens the neurological pathways to the subconscious where real learning takes place.

And speaking of learning we come to the most prominent and visible aspect of the Adult Ego: The exchange of information. Adults Egos collect, store, retrieve, and freely trade information. Like Mr. Spock of *Star Trek*, our Adult Egos are a wonderful human encyclopedia of information. Simply request information and out it comes. Perhaps some of life's most pleasurable moments are caused by the meaningful exchange of information. This is what school is really about. It is the time spent with other learners and master learners (teachers) for the specific purpose of feeding information to our ever hungry, ever questing Adult Ego States.

Somehow we ran afoul of the true learning purpose by focusing on the form of school rather than the content. We have become so consumed with the way things **should** run (Parent Ego) that we forgot that school form needs to follow school function (Adult Ego) because the sole function is to provide our students and ourselves with as much information about the way the world works as is possible. Instead, we have meetings about having too many meetings. And, of course, we strike. We'll punish those ungrateful communities who pay us a pitance, our Parent Ego says. We'll show you how much you need us! Instead of using the power, which is very weak (look at your paycheck, teacher), of our Parent Egos, we are learning (finally) the real and awesome power of our Adults. By sending home letters congratulating parents on the achievements of their children, we sensitize our communities to the great jobs we are doing. Now when the bond issue goes to the voters, it passes.

I must say that in most of the school districts where I have served as a consultant on discipline (more than two thousand), the teachers do not strike. They work harder. But the point of the hard work carries a specific message to the community, which when you know how (Adult), is very easy to do. With the community morale high on the job the schools are doing, and the teacher moral high, too, long overdue salary hikes are obtained **easily**.

In so many school districts throughout America today a Parent Ego-Child Ego relationship exists between the district administrators and the teaching staff. This destructive relationship borders more on paternalism than professionalism. One administrator in a state which I shall not name said (and I quote) "We don't have no union here, no sir. We're just one big happy family." After talking to some of his teachers, I discovered that his notion of "happy family" was as faulty as his grammar. Remember, please, that the Adult Ego does not win at the expense of others. The Adult Ego realizes that life is **not** like sports. In sports one wins because someone else loses. In life if I win at your expense, I lose because you will not do business with me again. The Parent Ego fails to understand this concept.

The concept of sharing is fundamental to the full expression of the Adult Ego. For instance. I think it is an excellent illustration of the lack of common sense in child rearing that people in my profession get paid for running around the nation telling parents to spend "quality time" with their children. This demonstrates how pervasive the Parent Ego has become. Of course, the Adult Ego **knows** experientially and emotionally what joy there is in conversing with children. The Adult Ego further understands that exchanging information with the Adult Ego of children is the very definition of the overworked and hopelessly inadequate phrase "quality time." Put another way, if you have little or no Adult Ego, then you can forget "quality time" with your children or students because you are only going to experience it by accident. What I am saying here is that your Adult Ego State can engineer specifically and at virtually any time "quality time" and you don't need large blocks of time to do it. But if it only happens by accident, you need lots of time for it to happen.

I engineer "quality time" (I am not fond of the phrase — can you tell?) every day in my office with my young patients. I only have a limited framework of time in which to work. Do they look forward to seeing me?

Do they open up and tell me everything?

Do they trust me, and draw for me, and play *Star Trek* with me?

Do they beg for the Vulcan mind meld?

Do they cry when they have to go and do they want to come see me tomorrow? Lord, yes, yes, yes.

All this because I stay in my Adult Ego with them **all** the time. Even when they hang on the cuckoo clock chains? Yes. I say, "Michael, you are making a bad choice." He looks at me. He says, "Will you make Fred come out?" (Fred is the cuckoo.)

I say, "First we finish our work without interruption and then Fred will come out on his own."
"OK."
"Thank you, Michael. I love to see your cooperation. You will be an excellent labor negotiator some day."
"Thank you."
"You are welcome, Michael."
"Dr. Zink?"
"Yes, partner?"
"What's a negotiator. Does he fly in a plane?"
"No. That's a navigator. A negotiator is someone who helps both sides get what they want."
"You mean like my dad when my mom is mad at me."
"You got it, partner. You have a wonderfully quick mind."
"Dr. Zink?"
"Yes, Michael?"
"Do you think I'm smart enough to be a doctor like you someday?"
"I certainly do. No question about it."
"How do I become a doctor?"
"Well, Michael, you use your imagination. Just close your eyes and pretend with all your might that you are a doc-

tor. See yourself all grown up in your office seeing all of your patients. Give your patients names, give their problems special names, and listen to yourself as you help them solve their problems. Listen very, very hard to what they tell you because always they will give the answers to their problems all by themselves."

"You mean they already know the answers to their problems? What do they need me for?"

"Good question, Michael. See what a great doctor you will be? Great doctors always ask questions just like you. The answer to your question is that your patients need you to love them, respect them, and to teach them to feel good about themselves."

"But I can do that now."

"See what a fine doctor you have become. Oh-oh. There's Fred."

"I know," Michael says as he leaves, "He's the only cuckoo one in your office!"

We both laugh. All this from a seven year-old boy who was diagnosed as having attention deficit disorder with hyperactivity and who, until he started working with me, was being given 2mg of Ritalin every day for 18 months. When I requested that his pediatrician stop the Ritalin and that we try a new approach, the physician said, "Ok, but good luck. He tears up my office every time he comes in here. Frankly, the girls in the office can't stand him."

Now we see why he tears up the office.

Perhaps the most fundamental aspect of the Adult Ego is the recognition that we all have the need to love and be loved. The Adult Ego recognizes that we are all very much the same in our needs. If you are lonely, unhappy, or depressed, it is largely because your Parent Ego State has imprisoned you inside a confining and unpleasent cell of your own making. The Adult Ego is the key to unlocking that cell. By being warm and friendly to yourself, you become an asset to yourself. This helps you hoist a sign to the world which reads, "I am a lovable person." Once your sign is out, others will read it and be attracted to you. It doesn't matter how fantastic a physical form you possess (a nice one helps, of course), nor does it matter how much education you have earned (the more the better to be sure), nor does it really matter if you have money or not (money does help, I believe), but what does matter is how you can love yourself. For if you can not truly love yourself, it is unreasonable (intellectually **and** emotionally) to expect others to love you.

Let me teach this to you **emotionally** by referring to one of my very favorite stories from *The Bible*. Now some people (God help them) are turned-off when the Bible is mentioned, but that is because some Parent Ego State punished them by **forcing** them to read it ("You **should** read your Bible in church and every day, honey.").

This is sad that these regressions to the Child Ego State take place when someone mentions *The Bible* because the book contains a great storehouse of human wisdom.

I call your attention to the story of the woman who was caught by the townspeople in adultery. There she was backing up in the street with terror in her eyes because advancing upon her was a mob of outraged citizens who had stones in their hands, justice on their minds, and murder in their hearts. Their laws had been violated and, by God, this little Jezebel was going to be punished.

Now as she backs into the wall which ends the street, shrinking from the parental hand of retribution as surely as a child who is about to get smacked holds high her hands to stave the blow, from a side street comes a man. He does not pick up a rock, he does not leap out and challenge the mob to stop this idiocy now. These actions would be very Parent Ego and would not accomplish his task. Instead, and to the amazement of all, he kneels down in the street and begins to write in the dust with his finger.

Here we have this perfectly angered and justifiably enfuriated crowd, about to legally carry out the letter of the law, and this character is writing something in the street. They keep looking at that finger wondering what he is writing. If he wasn't a hypnotist, this man knew the basic principles. He diverted their attention and changed the collective emotion of the moment. Then, with one sentence as he faced the crowd from his crouched position in the street, he put them all into their Adult Ego States.

"Let he who is without sin cast the first stone."

One by one we see them take a deep breath, sigh, and realizing the consummate power of the **permission to make a bad choice** he gave them, they returned their stones to the street and walked away. They made good choices.

This would be a great illustration of the power of the adult, but the story teller makes it the finest example in all literature of the power of the Adult Ego.

The man looks up to see the mob has gone. Then he looks at the woman. Can you imagine the look of love in her eyes? Then, this wonderful adult, like all Adult Egos, asks for information. He says, "Woman, where are thy accusers?"

She, in her adult, now, replies with information. She says, "They are gone, Lord."

She, in her adult, now, replies with information. She says, "They are gone, Lord."

Please notice the term, "Lord." It is a positive message, clearly the sign of the Adult Ego, and wouldn't you in the same circumstance call him "Lord" too? Then the man speaks the perfect line which articulates the seminal concept of the triumph of the Adult Ego.

"Then you go, too. For neither will I condemn you."

Forgiveness is the message of the Adult Ego State. Forgiveness for ourselves and the forgiveness for others, after all, is His message.

It strikes me as somehow worthy of note that the old testament of *The Bible* presents a God in his Parent Ego State. He is angry, throwing Adam and Eve out, burning Sodom and Gomorrah, flooding the world, promising no more disasters ("Mommy is sorry she hit you. She will never do it again!") and then running the Israelites all over forty miles of desert for forty years, killing Pharoah's soldiers, and bringing pestilence as punishment. The old testament is a book of punishment, really. "My God is a mighty God of war," the Psalmist says. In the old testament we find *Lex Talionis*, the eye for an eye philosphy and, curiously enough, the one Bible passage cited by all who need to justify their physical abuse of children, "Spare the rod and spoil the child."

Now the new testament of *The Bible* is a book of love and forgiveness. "Love thy neighbor as thyself," the man says. And please note the importance of the words , "**as thyself.**"

This man, a teacher, also taught us to "turn the other cheek." Incredible. Did the Parent Ego God of the old testament **ever** turn the other cheek? Never. He wore himself out zapping people.

Even when the man of the new testament has a justifiably human right to be angry and display His Parent Ego (even He had one) He takes the cords from around His cloak and runs through the temple chasing the money-changers. I am sure He forgave Himself for this weak moment of Parent Ego anger. I like to think that episode is described to teach us that we all slip from time to time. And this man had a Child Ego, too. Did He not say, "Father, if it be possible, let this chalice pass from me"? In other words, "Don't make me do it, Daddy. Don't make me do it."

But in the end, His adult triumphed and this is why we remember Him two thousand years later. For as He died for His friends, He said of His enemies, "Father, forgive them for they know not what they do." And He was so very right. They didn't. The Parent Ego never does.

NOTES

EPILOGUE

"They know not what they do." The line does explain the Parent Ego, doesn't it? Do parents and teachers realize the full extent of the damage we do to our children? Do we realize that what we say and do deeply and profoundly affects their emotional well-being? Do we realize the thunderous power we possess to shape or scar their lives?

I think not. But perhaps after reading this little book of mine you are more aware of your choices. You have three, essentially. Each corresponds to a different Ego State and because the word "ego" is Latin for first person singular, we can all choose which "I" we want to be.

Is it the tyrannical "I" who am appointed by God Almighty to point out all the stupid, dumb, insane, and idiotic things the children in my classroom or home do and say?

Is it the defensive "I" who feels mostly like crying because life isn't fair and why does this always happen to me? I'm ok, aren't I? Tell me I'm ok. Tell me everything is going to be all right. Please!

Or is it the loving "I" who intends to live my own life to the best of my abilities and live up to no one's expectations but my own while giving others the right to define and live up to their own?

You see, my friends and colleagues, there really are choices in life and each of us must choose.

Whatever choice you make is ok. I accept your choice even as I accept you. And if after reading my book, you choose to remain in your parent (or child) ego, that is acceptable to me. I can't change you. You know that now if you didn't before.

But as an adult, I can provide you with the information to make an informed choice. And this I have done, to the best of my ability. In writing this book I realize that there may be mistakes and flaws in my thinking here. These I accept and forgive myself for because under the circumstances I know in my heart that I did the best job I could do given my age, education, and experience.

I have this good feeling about what I have done because I worked hard. And I believe that this work will bear fruit as yet unimagined by me or those who share my love.

Ultimately, whether or not I have made a good choice spending the hours to research and write this book will be determined by the minds and hearts of those who read it and choose.

And for the opportunity to give this gift of my time, energy, and love to you, I thank you in advance.

NOTES

APPENDIX A

The Workbook From
Dr. Zink's Workshop
On Positive Discipline.

Directions: Here is the workbook which parents and teachers in my workshops find most helpful. Carefully read each section and use this workbook to complete the first drafts of your Positive Discipline Plans. Remember, your Adult Ego is achieved by devising a plan, trying your plan, evaluating your plan's effectiveness, revising your plan according to all the information you have gathered, and periodically fine-tuning your plan as your needs change and the children develop.

One final note: The plan is **not** your Adult Ego State; it only helps you achieve your Adult Ego. The loving and positive choice to remain in your adult ego is up to you. **Go get'em!**

THE ZINK METHOD

Skill Number One: The Rules

First a word on the rules.

Without rules we would have no society. All systems of governance must include some form of code for human behavior. Primitive societies all have extremely well developed codes. So how can you run your classroom *or* your home without rules? The answer is you cannot. You must have rules. Must.

However, as you are about to learn (like the Emperor Justinian and King Henry the Second of England before you) writing a useful set of rules is a little more difficult than it first sounds.

So, because you are not the first teacher or parent to need some good rules, I have constructed a comprehensive set of guidelines for you to follow while you are writing your rules. *Do not deviate* from the guidelines unless you have a very, very good reason!

Guidelines

The Rules

1. Keep them short and to the point.

2. Write them in the language of kids.

3. Never use more than five. Ever.

4. Cover all contingencies in five rules.

5. Meet your needs first.

6. Revise rules whenever necessary.

7. Post all rules, prices, and positive messages.

8. Both parents must agree on all rules (for home).

9. Personally present the rules (and plan) to the kids.

THE RULES FOR MY CLASSROOM

1. _____

_____

2. _____

_____

3. _____

_____

4. _____

_____

5. _____

_____

SAMPLE CLASSROOM RULES

PLEASE NOTE: These are samples *only*. The very best rules are the ones you write all by yourself.

1. Follow directions the first time I give them. No exceptions.

2. Raise your hand and wait for me to call on you.

3. Keep your hands, feet, books, pencils, and other objects to yourself.

4. Return all materials to their proper place when you are finished with them.

5. Be in your seat, ready to work, when the bell rings.

6. No swearing, cussing, teasing, or obscene gestures at any time.

7. My permission and a pass must be granted before you may leave the classroom.

8. Come to class prepared—with books, pencils, paper, and homework.

9. Remain in your seat unless I give you permission to leave it.

10. No food, gum, or candy during class.

THE RULES FOR MY HOME:

1. _____

_____

2. _____

_____

3. _____

_____

4. _____

_____

5. _____

_____

SAMPLE HOME RULES

PLEASE NOTE: These are samples *only*. The very best rules are the ones you (and your spouse) write together! (None of this "You write a draft, Honey, and I'll check it over.)

1. Follow directions the first time I say them. No backtalk.

2. No teasing or name calling.

3. Return toys to their proper place as soon as you are finished playing with them.

4. Wash hands and face and brush teeth before coming to breakfast.

5. Get up, dress, and be ready to leave on time for school.

6. Make your bed and pick-up your clothes before leaving for school.

7. Notify us by phone when you are out and you change locations.

8. Be home by (10, 11, 12, etc.) or call before then with the reason why you will be late.

9. Do not borrow from or lend your things to others.

10. Do your homework as soon as you get home from school.

THE ZINK METHOD

Skill Number Two: The Prices

My method works if you remember this important observation about life: *For every bad choice you have to pay a price*. Always. There are no exceptions. But prices are *not* punishments. A punishment is when someone makes you feel bad about yourself as a person. Punishments are demeaning and they ruin self-esteem. A price, on the other hand, is just something you have to do or pay because you made a bad choice. There are two kinds of prices—artificial prices and natural prices. Artificial prices are set up by those in authority to teach others not to make bad choices. Example: Driving drunk is a bad choice. The artificial price is the possible loss of your license and maybe jail and a fine. The natural price is a bad liver and maybe death for someone else or you.

REMEMBER: There are no good or 'bad' kids in my method. Just kids who make good or bad choices. And when they make a bad choice, they pay the price. Every single time.

Guidelines

The Prices

1. To break a rule is to pay a price, *always*.

2. Prices are not punishment. Punishment ruins self-esteem.

3. Boredom is a good price. Kids hate to be bored.

4. Arrange prices in an ascending order of severity. Start mild, get stronger.

5. If a price is not working, use something stronger. Never hit, never yell.

6. When giving a price for a bad choice, never lose your cool.

7. Never take a child's bad choice personally. Kids have a right to make a bad choice.

8. Never use the loss of a reward as a price. This makes a Catch-2 situation.

9. Prices are the weakest part of a positive discipline program.

SAMPLE PRICES FOR CLASSROOM

1. Verbal warning.

2. Detention time after school.

3. Detention time before school.

4. Call to parents.

5. Sent to another teacher's room for a short time.

6. Last one to be dismissed.

7. Playground pick-up.

8. In-school suspension.

9. All behavior tape recorded and played for parents.

10. Extra assignments and/or taken to father's or mother's place of business.

THE PRICES FOR MY CLASSROOM:

1. _____

_____

2. _____

_____

3. _____

_____

4. _____

_____

5. _____

_____

The price for a "major" bad choice is: _____

_____

My definition of a "major" bad choice is: _____

_____

SAMPLE PRICES FOR HOME

1. Penalty box for a short time.

2. Loss of television time for a short time.

3. Loss of telephone time for a short time.

4. Loss of the right to have a friend over to play for a day.

5. Bed after dinner.

6. Loss of a favorite toy for a short time.

7. May not use the car for the rest of the week.

8. Loss of special favors—like rides to and from places to which they could walk.

9. (If the problem is serious) Mandatory time with a counselor or involvement with a special program (like drug and alcohol abuse centers).

10. Loss of the stereo or radio for a short time and then a longer time.

THE PRICES FOR MY HOME:

1. _____

   _____

2. _____

   _____

3. _____

   _____

4. _____

   _____

5. _____

   _____

And if these are not working, I will use these:

1. _____

   _____

2. _____

   _____

3. _____

   _____

And if these do not work, I will think of something else
because my kids are too important for me to quit.

Notes

THE ZINK METHOD

Skill Number Three: Positive Messages

You hear a lot these days about positive reinforcement. There is even talk about "strokes." I don't like the term "positive reinforcement" because it makes our job of raising and teaching children sound like we are conducting laboratory experiments with pigeons and rats. Our children are not pigeons and rats! The term "strokes" nauseates me.

I like the phrase "Positive Message" because it is as close to "I Love You" and "I Care For You" as I can get and still sound like a behavioral psychologist and not a love poet. But keep this in mind: a positive message is a lot more than a simple reinforcer or a "stroke." Also remember that if you *master* this skill, you do not need the first two that I taught you. Because this one contains all the power on the face of the earth. The trick is in learning how to *use* it.

Guidelines

Positive Messages

1. Catch them doing something right!

2. Make your body say what your mouth is saying.

3. Put your energy and emotion into it. If you do not mean it, don't say it.

4. Once is not enough. Say it over and over and over.

5. Be *very* specific with your praise. Positive messages really say "I love you."

6. Remember that what you praise is what you will get.

7. Material rewards can be positive messages. They are not "bribes."

8. Don't substitute material rewards for your genuine emotion.

9. When using the reward systems, make sure they can win. Always stack the deck *for* them when using reward system.

SAMPLE POSITIVE MESSAGES FOR MY CLASSROOM:

1. Verbal praise—sincere and specific.

2. Positive non-verbal praise.

3. Five minutes of music at the end of class.

4. Extra P.E. time.

5. End of the week grab bag drawing.

6. Cut passes to go to the head of the line anywhere in the school.

7. The right to miss an assignment without penalty.

8. A telephone call to the parents explaining an outstanding job.

9. Letters of praise and awards of achievement sent to parents and grandparents.

10. A Polaroid photograph taken of the youngster and his/her friend.

THE POSITIVE MESSAGES FOR MY CLASSROOM:

1. _____

_____

2. _____

_____

3. _____

_____

4. _____

_____

5. _____

_____

The classwide reward for my classroom is _____

_____

The alternative classwide reward is _____

_____

SAMPLE POSITIVE MESSAGES FOR MY HOME:

(REMEMBER: These are samples only. Come up with your own!)

1.   Sincere verbal praise.

2.   Positive non-verbal praise.

3.   Earn a special toy or article of clothing.

4.   Earn "special time" with mom or dad with absolutely no interruptions.

5.   Earn extra television or telephone time.

6.   Earn a special family field trip, gathering, or adventure.

7.   Earn extra use of the family car.

8.   Earn the right to have friends over to spend the night.

9.   Special phone calls to grandparents and significant others to share in the special achievement.

10. The opportunity to take mom or dad to dinner to say "Thank You For Being You."

THE POSITIVE MESSAGES FOR MY HOME:

1. _____

_____

2. _____

_____

3. _____

_____

4. _____

_____

5. _____

_____

The family-wide reward is _____

_____

The ultimate family-wide reward is _____

_____

THE CHAMPIONS SERIES
by
Dr. J. Zink

BOOK ONE: $9.95
Praised by teachers and parents as the most straight-forward and easy to read approach to positive discipline, **Building Positive Self-Concept in Kids** will give you hundreds of good ideas for making your relationship with kids a positive experience. This book will train you to build a step-by-step positive discipline plan.

BOOK TWO: $9.95
Motivation problems? Discipline problems? Drug, Alcohol & Teen Sex problems? This book will give you answers! Written in an easy-to-understand style, **Motivating Kids** will give you novel and effective solutions to the bewildering array of troubles that parents and teachers face today.

BOOK THREE: $9.95
EGO STATES is the culmination of the champions trilogy. Here Dr. Zink explains why we lose our tempers, harbor anger, and engage in self-destructive behaviors which further erode our self-esteem. Here are the EXACT steps to take to become more loving and feel more competent as parents and teachers. Whatever you do, don't miss this one!

DEARLY BELOVED: SECRETS OF SUCCESSFUL MARRIAGE $19.95-(Hardbound Only)
Working on the theme of three parts in marriage (sex, intimacy, and commitment) and drawing on his experience in private practice, Dr. Zink departs from his usual subject of child behavior to focus on marriage. Written to celebrate their 21st wedding anniversary, **Dearly Beloved** includes commentory by Dr. Zink's wife, Kern. Here are their secrets of their successful marriage spelled out in plain talk. Don't be married without it!

THE AUDIO TAPE: $14.95

Hear Dr. Zink explain how certain messages destroy and certain messages build a positive self-concept in children and young adults. A motivating and emotional experience, this one hour tape will get you charged up and on a positive track for getting kids to behave. This tape will teach you to follow-through on a positive discipline plan for home or school.

Video Tape One For Parents: The Rules $34.95

Here Dr. Zink describes the very specifics that positive parents use to write the rules for the behavior of their children. This no-nonsense approach includes help for divorced and blended families. (VHS only)

Video Tape Two For Parents: The Prices $34.95

This tape teaches what positive parents do and say when the kids break the rules. Prices are not punishment, Dr. Zink shows clearly, and when you learn this special skill, you are on your way to being a positive parent. (VHS only)

Video Tape Three For Parents: The Positives $34.95

Catching our kids following the rules is what we all know we should do. Here Dr. Zink shares the secrets of the most positive parents as they develop a loving, positive, and powerfully fulfilling relationship with their children. It is never too late to begin! (VHS only)

Video Tape Four For Parents: The Zink Money System $34.95

Thousands of parents have been thrilled with the remarkable effectiveness of this system which replaces allowances for kids with an efficient method for teaching the value of money while building self-worth. (VHS only)

Video Tape Five For Teachers: Classroom Discipline $99.95

Here is the tape educators have been waiting for! Eighty minutes crammed with hundreds of useful ideas organized into a simple system for effective classroom discipline! No one can motivate teachers like Dr. J. Zink. (VHS only)

Video Tape Six For Teachers: The Most Asked Questions On Discipline. $99.95

In this live session, today's classroom teachers ask Dr. Zink many of the penetrating and very relevant questions facing educators concerned with discipline. Witty and poignant, some of Dr. Zink's answers may surprise even veterans. (VHS only)

THE COMPLETE CHAMPIONS WORKSHOP AUDIO TAPE: $49.95

And introducing for the first time ever, the complete Dr. J. Zink CHAMPIONS WORKSHOP on audio tape! **Three hours** of fun and fulfillment. On March 5th, 1986, Dr. Zink gave what many consider to be the finest workshop of his professional life to 500 educators in La Porte, Indiana. Here, for the first time, is the complete sound track to that workshop. Dr. Zink, in his own humorous style, teaches his EN-TIRE POSITIVE DISCIPLINE PROGRAM on high quality audio cassettes. You will laugh, cry, and learn how to get YOUR needs met while raising and teaching kids!

THE ZINK BULLSEYE CHART: $9.95

Here is the famous Bullseye Chart that has proven so effective in raising academic and behavior performance in kids. 22X34 inches, this plastic-coated, **reusable** progress grade chart teaches kids how to track their own progress. It is ready to hang on the back of their bedroom doors and raise those grades!

THE GUIDES: $3.95 (each)

Champions on the School Bus and **Champions in the Library**. These guides for positive discipline were written specifically for school bus drivers and librarians. In very clear language, these unique pamphlets describe specific techniques to help kids feel good about themselves for behaving on the bus and in the library. No school bus and no library should be without one.

You will believe you can make champions.

Dr. Zink, please send:

_____ Copy(s) BOOK I (Self-Concept)	@	$ 9.95	= $ _____
_____ Copy(s) BOOK II (Motivation)	@	$ 9.95	= $ _____
_____ Copy(s) BOOK III (Ego States)	@	$ 9.95	= $ _____
_____ Copy(s) DEARLY BELOVED (Secrets of Successful Marriage)	@	$19.95	= $ _____
_____ Copy(s) CHAMPIONS AUDIO TAPE	@	$14.95	= $ _____
_____ Copy(s) CHAMPIONS VIDEO TAPES	@	$ _____	= $ _____
Specify Tape Numbers _____			
_____ Copy(s) THE COMPLETE CHAMPIONS WORKSHOP AUDIO TAPE	@	$49.95	= $ _____
_____ Copy(s) SCHOOL BUS	@	$ 3.95	= $ _____
_____ Copy(s) LIBRARY	@	$ 3.95	= $ _____
_____ Copy(s) ZINK BULLSEYE CHART	@	$ 9.95	= $ _____

Total Cost of Material Ordered $ _____

Shipping & Handling (10% of total cost; $2.50 min.) $ _____

Shipping & Hanldling outside U.S.A. (10% of total cost; $5.00 min.) $ _____

CA Residents only: Add 6 ½ % of total cost $ _____

                              Total amount enclosed $ _____

ORDER MUST BE ACCOMPANIED BY PAYMENT IN FULL. SCHOC
DISTRICTS: PURCHASE ORDER IS OK.

Make check payable to:

> J. ZINK, INC.
> P.O. BOX 3279
> MANHATTAN BEACH, CA 90266

PLEASE SHIP MY MATERIALS TO: (PRINT)

_____

NAME

_____

STREET & ADDRESS

_____

CITY   STATE   ZIP

Note: For VIEDO TAPE VHS format only.